Independent Schools
Examinations Board

CLASSICAL GREEK
for Beginners

Kristian Waite

Independent Schools
Examinations Board

www.galorepark.co.uk

GALORE PARK

Published by ISEB Publications, an imprint of Galore Park Publishing Ltd
19/21 Sayers Lane, Tenterden, Kent TN30 6BW
www.galorepark.co.uk

Printed and bound in the UK by CPI Antony Rowe, Chippenham

ISBN-13 978 1 907047 13 8

First published 2002, reprinted 2009, 2011

Details of other ISEB Revision Guides for Common Entrance, examination
papers and Galore Park publications are available at www.galorepark.co.uk

Front cover photographs: © Julian Morgan 2009

CONTENTS

Introduction to the teacher 1

Introduction to the pupil 3

Chapter 1   The Greek alphabet – lower case 5

Chapter 2   The Greek alphabet – upper case 8

Chapter 3   The Greek alphabet – pronunciation 10

Chapter 4   The Greek alphabet – English to Greek 12

Chapter 5   The verb – present tense of $\lambda \upsilon \omega$ 14

            Vocabulary check-list 1 16

Chapter 6   Conjunctions and the negative 17

Chapter 7   The definite article

            The noun – 1st declension feminine nouns 18

            Vocabulary check-list 2 21

Chapter 8   The noun – 1st declension masculine nouns 22

            Vocabulary check-list 3 24

Chapter 9   The verb – present tense of $\epsilon \grave{\iota} \mu \iota$

            Use of the genitive sandwich 25

Chapter 10   Prepositions and questions 27

Chapter 11   The noun – 2nd declension masculine and

            feminine nouns 29

            Vocabulary check-list 4 31

Chapter 12   The noun – 2nd declension neuter nouns 32

            Vocabulary check-list 5 34

Chapter 13   The verb – imperfect tense of $\lambda \upsilon \omega$ 35

            Vocabulary check-list 6 37

Chapter 14   Adjectives 38

            Vocabulary check-list 7 41

Chapter 15   The verb – future tense of $\lambda \upsilon \omega$ 42

Practice unseen passages 44

Practice Common Entrance Level 1 paper 46

Grammar summary 48

Vocabulary 50

INTRODUCTION TO THE TEACHER

This book has been written in an attempt to produce a modern, concise, affordable and user-friendly resource for teachers of Greek in preparatory and senior schools. It is hoped that, as well as encouraging more interest in Greek at Common Entrance Level 1, this book may also prove of some use for pupils in the early stages of preparation for Common Entrance Level 2, scholarship and GCSE examinations. Its debt to existing coursebooks is obvious but, by concentrating exclusively on the vocabulary and grammatical requirements for Common Entrance Level 1 in a single volume, teachers and pupils may now find it considerably easier than before to focus learning and revision for the Common Entrance examination.

Pacing is very much up to the individual teacher. With a typical class, it might reasonably be expected that one chapter a week could be covered over a 45 minute period, although some teachers may wish to spend longer over some chapters. The format of the book also lends itself well to regular extra-curricular sessions with interested and well-motivated pupils, although it should be made clear at the start of the course that a regular element of preparation and practice is required.

Information on historical and cultural aspects of classical Greece lies beyond the scope of this book. The individual teacher will have his or her own interests here and should incorporate such details where appropriate.

I should like to express my gratitude to Alec Synge for his unfailing support of Greek at Hazlewood School (where I taught for many years), to Oliver Butler for his illustrations and to Tony Allen, Stephen Anderson, Bob Bass, Michael Bevington and Bruce McCrae for their advice and help in the preparation of the first edition. Any errors and omissions remain, of course, my sole responsibility. I should also like to thank all the pupils at Hazlewood School who worked through the drafts of this book with unfailing enthusiasm and who were a constant source of inspiration.

Kristian Waite
Caterham School

INTRODUCTION TO THE PUPIL

The aim of this course is to give you a straightforward introduction to Greek so that you may attempt the Common Entrance Level 1 Greek examination with confidence after fifteen weeks or so of study. This book will also give you a firm basis from which to tackle Common Entrance Level 2 and, ultimately, scholarship and GCSE examinations.

Don't be put off by the strange appearance of Greek letters. You will soon get used to them. In terms of the amount of work to be covered, Greek at Common Entrance Level 1 is as easy as any subject. Not only will you get the chance to learn the Greek alphabet, but, just as Latin provides us with the basis for many English words, so you will also be surprised at how many Greek words have entered our own language.

Our own civilization owes at least as great a debt to the ancient Greeks as it does to the Romans. In areas such as medicine, the theatre, philosophy, democracy, architecture, history, geography and mathematics, the Greeks set standards which we can, in many ways, hardly improve upon. By learning Greek, you will have the opportunity to stretch your own mind and develop the same sort of powers of observation and analysis which once made the Greeks so powerful.

As for ancient Greek being 'dead', go to Athens after finishing this book and you will be surprised how many words you can understand. The Greek language has changed less in two and a half thousand years than English has since Chaucer.

Good luck with the course. By offering Greek at Common Entrance, you will send a strong signal to your senior school that you are someone who can clearly think for yourself. In a competitive world, it is a skill which will help you long after your schooldays are over.

CHAPTER 1

THE GREEK ALPHABET – LOWER CASE

The first and most obvious obstacle in learning ancient Greek is understanding the Greek alphabet, which the Greeks still use today. The first few chapters of this book will help you to understand and remember how the alphabet works. There are twenty-four letters in the Greek alphabet, and for the time being you should concentrate on the lower case letters which are far more common than the upper case forms.

lower case	upper case	name	sound in English
α	A	alpha	a (as in *hat*)
β	B	beta	b
γ	Γ	gamma	g (as in *go*)
δ	Δ	delta	d
ε	E	epsilon	e (short, as in *get*)
ζ	Z	zeta	z, sd (as in *wis<u>d</u>om*)
η	H	eta	e (long, as in *h<u>ai</u>r*)
θ	Θ	theta	th
ι	I	iota	i
κ	K	kappa	c, k
λ	Λ	lambda	l
μ	M	mu	m
ν	N	nu	n
ξ	Ξ	xi	x
o	O	omicron	o (short, as in *got*)
π	Π	pi	p
ρ	P	rho	r
σ, ς	Σ	sigma	s (ς only at end of word)
τ	T	tau	t
υ	Υ	upsilon	u, y
φ	Φ	phi	ph
χ	X	chi	ch
ψ	Ψ	psi	ps
ω	Ω	omega	o (long, as in *bone*)

Writing practice

Using a pencil, practise writing down each of the Greek letters in your exercise book. Set them out in the pattern shown below, and write down each lower and upper case letter five times. For the moment, concentrate on recognising the lower case letters. Your teacher will help you to practise some of the more difficult letters and may also teach you to pronounce one or two of the letters in a different way from the list on page 5.

α	A	alpha	'a'	_____
β	B	beta	'b'	_____
γ	Γ	gamma	'g'	_____
δ	Δ	delta	'd'	_____
ϵ	E	epsilon	'e'	_____

A short 'e' sound, as in the English *get*.

ζ	Z	zeta	'z', 'sd'	_____

An awkward looking letter which needs careful practice.

η	H	eta	'e'	_____

A long 'e' sound, as in the English *hair*, be careful not to confuse this letter with the English letter 'n'.

θ	Θ	theta	'th'	_____
ι	I	iota	'i'	_____
κ	K	kappa	'c, k'	_____
λ	Λ	lambda	'l'	_____
μ	M	mu	'm'	_____
ν	N	nu	'n'	_____

Don't confuse this with the English letter 'v' and be careful when writing this so that you don't confuse it with 'υ' (upsilon).

ξ	Ξ	xi	'x'	_____

Another awkward looking letter which needs careful practice.

o	O	omicron	'o'	_____

A short 'o' sound, as in the English *got*.

π	Π	pi	'p'	_____
ρ	P	rho	'r'	_____

Be careful not to confuse this with the English letter 'p'.

σ, ς	Σ	sigma	's'	_____

'ς' is only used at the end of a word.

τ	T	tau	't'	_____
υ	Υ	upsilon	'u, y'	_____
ϕ	Φ	phi	'ph'	_____
χ	X	chi	'ch'	_____
ψ	Ψ	psi	'ps'	_____
ω	Ω	omega	'o'	_____

A long 'o' sound, as in the English _bone_; be careful not to confuse this with the English letter 'w'.

Diphthongs

A diphthong is where two vowels combine to form one sound. In Greek, there are seven vowels: α, ϵ, η, ι, o, υ and ω. Here's how to pronounce some common combinations:

$\alpha\iota$	as in _high_		$\eta\upsilon$	as in _feud_
$\alpha\upsilon$	as in _cow_		$o\iota$	as in _coin_
$\epsilon\iota$	as in _eight_		$o\upsilon$	as in _cool_
$\epsilon\upsilon$	as in _feud_			

It is very important that you learn how to recognise, write and pronounce each letter of the Greek alphabet as quickly as possible. Once you have practised the alphabet, have a go at the exercise below and see how much you can remember.

Exercise 1.1

The following Greek words are still used in English. What are they? You may need to make some small spelling changes.

1. $\kappa o \mu \mu \alpha$
2. $\beta \alpha \sigma \iota s$
3. $\mu \eta \lambda o \nu$
4. $\mu \alpha \nu \iota \alpha$
5. $\chi \alpha o s$
6. $\kappa \alpha \nu \omega \nu$
7. $\phi o \iota \nu \iota \xi$
8. $\pi \alpha \nu \theta \eta \rho$
9. $\nu \epsilon \kappa \tau \alpha \rho$
10. $\pi \alpha \rho \alpha \lambda \upsilon \sigma \iota s$

Try to remember how to recite the Greek alphabet from alpha to omega before leaving this chapter, and see how many of the lower case letters you can recognise without having to look them up.

CHAPTER 2

THE GREEK ALPHABET – UPPER CASE

In this chapter, we'll be learning how to recognise capital letters in Greek. First though, it's time to find out what the Greeks used in place of the letter 'h', the absence of which you may have noticed when you first met the alphabet.

Breathings

When a Greek word begins with a vowel, a mark called a breathing is always written above it.

A **rough breathing** adds an 'h' sound to the start of a word and is shown by this mark ʽ over the top of the vowel. For example, the word $ἱστορια$ would be pronounced *historia*.

A **smooth breathing** is shown by this mark ʼ over the top of the vowel. It indicates the absence of the sound 'h'. For example, the word $ἰρις$ would be pronounced *iris*.

Exercise 2.1

All these Greek words, which are still used in English, have breathings. Write them out in English, and say whether the breathing in each is a smooth or rough one.

1. $ἰδεα$
2. $ἠχω$
3. $ἀσθμα$
4. $ἡρωες$
5. $ἠλεκτρον$

6. $ὁριζων$
7. $ἀκροπολις$
8. $ἰσοσκελης$
9. $ἀσβεστος$
10. $ἱπποποταμος$

Capital letters

As in English, capital letters are used to begin the names of people and places. However, they are **not** used to begin each sentence. Make sure that you can identify them, as in the Common Entrance Level 1 examination you will need to convert some names written in Greek letters into their English equivalents.

Breathings are written to the left of capital vowels. The Greek word for *Athens*, for example, is $Ἀθηναι$, pronounced *Athenai*. When a word begins with a diphthong, the breathing goes over the second vowel. For example, the Greek word for *Egypt* is $Aἰγυπτος$, pronounced *Aiguptos*.

Take care with the Greek capital eta, which looks like 'H' in Greek, but is pronounced 'E' in English.

Exercise 2.2

The following characters are famous from Greek mythology. Write them down in English. You may need to make some small spelling changes.

1. Ἄρης
2. Ἀθηνα
3. Ἥρα
4. Θησευς
5. Ἑρμης
6. Ἀπολλων

7. Ποσειδων
8. Ὀδυσσευς
9. Ἀφροδιτη
10. Κυκλωψ
11. Ἡρακλης
12. Προμηθευς

Exercise 2.3

Sometimes you will be asked questions about people or places whose spellings you will be less familiar with. Take care to write down these less well known names precisely and correctly.

1. Κορινθος
2. Σπαρτη
3. Κυπρος
4. Σαλαμις
5. Ἰβηρια
6. Ἀλεξανδρια

7. Σολων
8. Ξερξης
9. Εὐριπιδης
10. Ἡροδοτος
11. Θεμιστοκλης
12. Δημοσθενης

Try to make sure that you can identify and pronounce all the Greek capital letters correctly by the end of this chapter. You should also check that you know what a breathing looks like, and understand what difference a smooth or rough breathing can make to the sound of a Greek word.

CHAPTER 3

THE GREEK ALPHABET – PRONUNCIATION

By now, you should have become pretty confident on how to pronounce Greek letters in both their lower case and capital forms. In this chapter, we are going to give you practice in pronouncing some real Greek words. First though, some final language points.

Iota subscript

You will sometimes notice that when an iota (ι) follows α, η or ω, it is written underneath and is hardly sounded at all – so we get α, η and ω. This is called an iota subscript, and you will mostly encounter it with some nouns which you will meet later.

Double gamma

When two gammas ($\gamma\gamma$) are found in a word, they are pronounced 'ng' in English. For example, the Greek word for *I announce* is $\mathring{\alpha}\gamma\gamma\epsilon\lambda\lambda\omega$, pronounced *angello*, from which we get the English word *angel*.

Pronunciation practice

Here are some Greek words which you should now be able to pronounce. If you are in any doubt how to pronounce any of these words, consult the alphabet list in Chapter 1 and make sure that you have learnt how to recognise and pronounce all the lower case letters of the Greek alphabet before you go any further.

Exercise 3.1

Pronounce each of these Greek words and answer the questions which accompany them.

1. $\lambda\upsilon\omega$ (*I set free*)

2. $\gamma\rho\alpha\phi\omega$ (*I write*)
   Can you think of any English words which derive from this word?

3. $\lambda\epsilon\gamma\omega$ (*I say*)

4. $\sigma\tau\rho\alpha\tau\epsilon\upsilon\omega$ (*I march*)
   Can you think of any English words which derive from this word?

5. $\lambda\alpha\mu\beta\alpha\nu\omega$ (*I capture*)

6. $\mathring{\epsilon}\chi\omega$ (*I have*)
   What do we call the mark above the epsilon? Is it smooth or rough? What difference, if any, does it make to the sound of the word?

7. δουλος (*slave*)

8. χωρα (*country*)

9. ζῳον (*animal*)

   Note that this word has an iota subscript. Can you think of any English words which derive from this word?

10. πολιτης (*citizen*)

    Can you think of any English words which derive from this word?

11. ἱππος (*horse*)

    What do we call the mark above the iota? Is it smooth or rough? What difference, if any, does it make to the sound of the word?

12. ποταμος (*river*)

Exercise 3.2

The following story contains many Greek words which are still used in English today. Read the passage and write down, **in English letters**, the Greek words as they come up.

τραυμα in the city

One day, we decided to explore the μητροπολις. In the afternoon, we saw the ὀρχηστρα and in the evening we went to the κινημα to watch a δραμα. There was a terrible κλιμαξ for a member of the audience. We thought that he had fallen into a κωμα but a doctor there gave a διαγνωσις. After a careful ἀναλυσις of the symptoms, he said that the γενεσις of the patient's illness had been βακτηρια picked up on a trip to a tropical ζωνη. Eventually, the κρισις passed, though it could have been a καταστροφη for the poor man. He was certainly an odd χαρακτηρ and it was a very strange σκηνη for us all to have witnessed.

Well done if you have worked out the story without going back to check any of the letters! Before moving on, you must make sure that you can identify and pronounce any letter of the Greek alphabet in both its lower case and capital form.

CHAPTER 4

THE GREEK ALPHABET – ENGLISH TO GREEK

You have now had a good deal of practice in converting words written in Greek letters into their English equivalents. In the Common Entrance examination, you will also be required to convert simple English words into Greek letters. This chapter will give you plenty of help and advice with this sort of question.

Converting vowels into Greek letters

Write out again, if you need to, the lower case letters of the Greek alphabet shown in Lesson 1. You must feel confident both in writing out Greek letters and knowing which Greek letter to use for each English letter before attempting Exercise 4.1.

If a word begins with the English letter 'h' then you must place a rough breathing (ʽ) over the first vowel. *hydra*, for example, would become $\dot{v}\delta\rho\alpha$.

If a word begins with a vowel, but there is no 'h' sound, then you must place a smooth breathing (ʼ) over that vowel. *aristos*, for example, would become $\dot{\alpha}\rho\iota\sigma\tau o\varsigma$.

If a word begins with a diphthong, or two vowels sounded together, then the breathing is put on the second vowel. For example, *automaton* would become $\alpha\dot{v}\tau o\mu\alpha\tau o\nu$.

Words beginning with 'e' or 'o' can cause difficulty as these vowels have two forms each in Greek.
Short 'e' (marked e) in English is **epsilon** in Greek (ϵ).
Long 'e' (marked ē) in English is **eta** in Greek (η).
Short 'o' (marked o) in English is **omicron** in Greek (o).
Long 'o' (marked ō) in English is **omega** in Greek (ω).

Words beginning with rho (ρ) automatically have a rough breathing (ʽ) placed over the rho and are pronounced 'rh' in English. For example *rhododendron* would become $\dot{\rho}o\delta o\delta\epsilon\nu\delta\rho o\nu$.

The letter sigma is always written as 'σ' except at the end of a word when it should be written 'ς'.

Finally, remember that the Greek iota (ι) does not need to be dotted like the letter 'i' in English.

Exercise 4.1

Write the following words in Greek letters. Long vowels are marked for spelling where necessary.

1.	mega	6.	ethos	11.	psychē
2.	polis	7.	anemōne	12.	dēmocratia
3.	delta	8.	ōmega	13.	paragraphē
4.	choros	9.	stigma	14.	rhinocerōs
5.	alpha	10.	thōrax	15.	hydrophobia

Names of people and places

You will need to apply the same rules with the names of people and places, but bear in mind that the first letter will need to be a capital letter.

If the word begins with a vowel, the breathing goes to the left of it. *Atlas*, for example, would become Ἄτλας. If the word begins with a diphthong, then the breathing, as before, is put on the second vowel. *Aischylos*, for example, would become Αἰσχυλος.

Greek names beginning with 'J' will begin with a capital iota in their Greek forms. If a word begins with an iota, the breathing is always placed on the iota, even if the next letter is a vowel. The breathing is placed to the left of a capital iota. *Jasōn*, for example, would become Ἰασων.

Exercise 4.2

Write down the following people and places in Greek letters. Long vowels are marked for spelling where necessary.

1.	Zeus	6.	Helenē	11.	Italia
2.	Midas	7.	Petros	12.	Eurōpē
3.	Artemis	8.	Daphnē	13.	Olympia
4.	Hektōr	9.	Philippos	14.	Milētos
5.	Agamemnōn	10.	Jōsēphos	15.	Halikarnassos

You should now be able to convert individual Greek words into their English equivalents, and vice versa, with confidence. Both these skills are tested at Common Entrance Level 1. Do make sure that you can write down any Greek letter in either its lower case or capital form before you begin the next chapter.

CHAPTER 5

THE VERB – PRESENT TENSE OF $\lambda v \omega$

As in Latin, Greek verbs change their endings to indicate who is doing an action, and when it happened. In this chapter you will see how the present tense works in Greek.

Present tense endings

The present tense of $\lambda v \omega$, *I set free*, is easy to remember. All the verbs which you will meet at Common Entrance, except for one, end in '-ω' and change their present tense endings in the same way. Hyphens have been put in to show the present tense endings on the verb stem 'λv-'.

person	number	Greek verb	meaning
1st	singular	λv-ω	*I set free*
2nd	singular	λv-$\epsilon\iota\varsigma$	*you set free*
3rd	singular	λv-$\epsilon\iota$	*he / she / it sets free*
1st	plural	λv-$o\mu\epsilon\nu$	*we set free*
2nd	plural	λv-$\epsilon\tau\epsilon$	*you set free*
3rd	plural	λv-$ov\sigma\iota(\nu)$	*they set free*

The 3rd person plural form $\lambda v o v \sigma \iota \nu$ is used before a word beginning with a vowel or at the end of a sentence.

Try to memorise the present tense of $\lambda v \omega$ as quickly as possible. Note that Greek, like Latin, does not have to use a separate word for *I*, *you* etc.

Exercise 5.1

Practise saying the present tenses of the following verbs in full. They all copy the pattern of $\lambda v \omega$. Hyphens have been included to show you where the endings should be added.

1. $\dot{\alpha}\gamma$-ω (*I lead*)
2. $\gamma\rho\alpha\phi$-ω (*I write*)
3. $\dot{\epsilon}\chi$-ω (*I have*)
4. θv-ω (*I sacrifice*)
5. $\pi\alpha v$-ω (*I stop*)
6. $\sigma\tau\rho\alpha\tau\epsilon v$-$\omega$ (*I march*)

Once you have learnt the present tense of λυω it soon becomes easy to apply the endings to other verbs which you will learn during the course. This skill is tested at Common Entrance Level 1, where you will be asked to translate a selection of basic verbs with different present tense endings.

Exercise 5.2

Translate these verbs into English. Check the endings carefully before answering. The basic meaning of the verb is in brackets.

1. ἀγ-εις   (lead)
2. γραφ-ομεν   (write)
3. ἐχ-ουσι   (have)
4. θυ-ει   (sacrifice)
5. παυ-ετε   (stop)
6. στρατευ-ω   (march)
7. ἀγ-ομεν   (lead)
8. θυ-ετε   (sacrifice)
9. παυ-ει   (stop)
10. γραφ-ω   (write)
11. στρατευ-ουσιν (march)
12. ἐχ-εις   (have)

When you are asked to translate single verb forms at Common Entrance, you will need to work out who is doing the action by looking at the verb ending, and apply this to your knowledge of the verb which you have learnt in its first person singular form.

Exercise 5.3

In this exercise some new verbs are introduced. Practise saying in full their present tenses and then translate each question. Be careful with endings, as the hyphens have been left out this time.

βαλλω = I throw
θεραπευω = I honour
λαμβανω = I capture

λεγω = I say
μενω = I remain
παιδευω = I train

1. βαλλει.
2. θεραπευουσι.
3. λαμβανομεν.
4. λεγεις.
5. μενετε.
6. παιδευομεν.
7. βαλλετε.
8. μενει.
9. παιδευεις.
10. λαμβανει.
11. λεγουσιν.
12. θεραπευομεν.

This is an important chapter. Go over it again carefully and, before proceeding further, memorise the present tense of λυω and learn, from Greek to English, the words listed in Vocabulary check-list 1 on the next page. These include a couple of new words which you will meet in Chapter 6.

Revise these words carefully from Greek to English before starting the next chapter.

ἀγω   I lead
γραφω   I write
ἐχω   I have, hold
θυω   I sacrifice
λυω   I set free
παυω   I stop
στρατευω   I march

και   and
ἀλλα / ἀλλ'   but
οὐ / οὐκ / οὐχ not

'I've caught a biggun!'

CHAPTER 6

CONJUNCTIONS AND THE NEGATIVE

This chapter will give you further practice on the verbs and present tense endings which you have just learnt, and will show you how to build sentences using the words *and*, *but* and *not*.

Conjunctions

καὶ = *and*

ἀλλα = *but*

ἀλλ' = *but* (before a vowel)

Exercise 6.1

All the verbs in this lesson are taken from Vocabulary check-list 1.

1. στρατευω καὶ ἀγω.
2. θυει ἀλλα γραφομεν.
3. ἀγετε καὶ θυετε.
4. στρατευουσι καὶ θυουσιν.
5. στρατευει καὶ λυει.
6. γραφω ἀλλα θυεις.

The negative

Greek has the following three ways of saying *not*:

οὐ = *not* (before consonants)

οὐκ = *not* (before vowels with **smooth** breathings)

οὐχ = *not* (before vowels with **rough** breathings)

Exercise 6.2

1. οὐ θυομεν.
2. οὐ στρατευεις.
3. οὐκ ἀγετε.
4. οὐκ ἐχουσιν.
5. οὐ θυω ἀλλα στρατευω.
6. οὐ γραφει ἀλλα θυει.
7. στρατευεις ἀλλ' οὐκ ἀγεις.
8. θυετε ἀλλ' οὐ στρατευετε.
9. γραφομεν ἀλλ' οὐ λυομεν.
10. ἀγεις ἀλλ' οὐ στρατευουσιν.

CHAPTER 7

THE DEFINITE ARTICLE
THE NOUN – 1ST DECLENSION FEMININE NOUNS

In this chapter we shall meet some nouns for the first time. First though, time to learn the various Greek words for *the*.

The definite article

Greek, unlike Latin, uses a separate word for *the*. This is called the **definite article**. In Greek, this word has many different forms, because it always indicates the gender, number and case of the noun to which it is attached. Although the definite article looks complicated, it is actually much easier to learn than it appears. It will also give you important information about the gender, number and case of the nouns which you will meet while learning Greek, which will make translation work much easier.

You should learn it across, singular first then plural.

	singular			plural		
	masc.	**fem.**	**neut.**	**masc.**	**fem.**	**neut.**
nom.	ὁ	ἡ	το	οἱ	αἱ	τα
acc.	τον	την	το	τους	τας	τα
gen.	του	της	του	των	των	των
dat.	τῳ	τῃ	τῳ	τοις	ταις	τοις

Noun cases

Every noun in Greek, like Latin, must be in a case which defines its role in the sentence. There are **five** noun cases in Greek.

nominative	–	used for the **subject** of the sentence
vocative	–	used for the person being **addressed**
accusative	–	used for the **object** of the sentence
genitive	–	used to express *of*
dative	–	used to express *to*, *for*, *by* and *with*

Nouns which are in the vocative case are generally introduced by ὦ (O) instead of the definite article.

1st declension feminine nouns

Greek, like Latin, divides nouns which have similar endings into groups called declensions. All the nouns which you will meet in this lesson are feminine in gender and belong to the 1st declension. Their nominative singular forms end in '-η' and '-α'.

Study carefully the examples below, and note how many of their endings copy those of the feminine part of the definite article.

		νικη	χωρα	θαλασσα
		victory	country	sea
singular				
nom.	ἡ	νικη	χωρα	θαλασσα
voc.	(ὠ)	νικη	χωρα	θαλασσα
acc.	την	νικην	χωραν	θαλασσαν
gen.	της	νικης	χωρας	θαλασσης
dat.	τῃ	νικῃ	χωρᾳ	θαλασσῃ
plural				
nom.	αἱ	νικαι	χωραι	θαλασσαι
voc.	(ὠ)	νικαι	χωραι	θαλασσαι
acc.	τας	νικας	χωρας	θαλασσας
gen.	των	νικων	χωρων	θαλασσων
dat.	ταις	νικαις	χωραις	θαλασσαις

Every noun with a nominative singular ending in '-η' which you will meet in this book has endings like νικη, and every noun with a nominative singular ending in '-α', with the exception of θαλασσα, has endings like χωρα.

nouns like νικη

γη	= land
ἐπιστολη	= letter
μαχη	= battle
φωνη	= voice
αἱ ’Αθηναι (pl.)	= Athens

nouns like χωρα

ἀγορα	= market-place
ἡμερα	= day
θεα	= goddess
οἰκια	= house
στρατια	= army

Greek has no separate word for *a* or *an*. ἡ νικη would mean *the victory*, but νικη by itself means *victory* or *a victory*.

Although there seems rather a lot to take in all at once in this chapter, you should concentrate on learning the definite article for the moment. Revise this thoroughly before trying Exercise 7.1.

Exercise 7.1

Give the number and case of the definite article in each of these phrases. Then translate the phrase. The basic meaning of each noun is given in brackets.

1.	ἡ ἀγορα	(market-place)	6.	τῶν οἰκιων	(house)
2.	της ἐπιστολης	(letter)	7.	τας ἡμερας	(day)
3.	αἱ μαχαι	(battle)	8.	ταις φωναις	(voice)
4.	τῃ γῃ	(land)	9.	αἱ στρατιαι	(army)
5.	τας θεας	(goddess)	10.	τῶν Ἀθηνων	(Athens)

Translation of sentences from Greek to English forms an important part of the Common Entrance examination. Unlike Latin, the word order in Greek is generally the same as in English, with verbs usually appearing in the middle of the sentence rather than at the end of it.

Exercise 7.2

The nouns in this exercise have all featured in this lesson and can also be found in Vocabulary check-list 2 on the next page.

1. ἀγω την στρατιαν.
2. παυεις την μαχην.
3. γραφομεν τας ἐπιστολας.
4. θυουσι τῃ θεᾳ.
5. ἐχεις οἰκιαν και γην.
6. ἡ θεα παυει την μαχην.
7. αἱ Ἀθηναι ἐχουσιν ἀγοραν.
8. ἡ στρατια οὐ λυει την χωραν.
9. γραφω την ἐπιστολην ἐν (in) τῃ οἰκιᾳ.
10. ἀγεις την στρατιαν προς (towards) την θαλασσαν.

This is another important chapter and you should not move on until you have understood its contents thoroughly. Before going any further, ensure that you have memorised the whole of the definite article and learnt, from Greek to English, the words listed in Vocabulary check-list 2 on the next page.

Vocabulary check-list 2

Revise these words carefully from Greek to English before starting the next chapter.

ἀγορα	(f.)	market-place
Ἀθηναι	(f. pl.)	Athens
γη	(f.)	land
ἐπιστολη	(f.)	letter
ἡμερα	(f.)	day
θαλασσα	(f.)	sea
θεα	(f.)	goddess
μαχη	(f.)	battle
νικη	(f.)	victory
οἰκια	(f.)	house
σοφια	(f.)	wisdom
στρατια	(f.)	army
φωνη	(f.)	voice
χωρα	(f.)	country
ὁ / ἡ / το		the
ὠ (+ voc.)		O

'Talk about a bad hair day!'

CHAPTER 8

THE NOUN – 1ST DECLENSION MASCULINE NOUNS

All the nouns which you met in the last chapter ended in '-η' or '-α' and were feminine in gender. Time now, to meet some very common masculine nouns and also to make sure that you can confidently identify the masculine parts of the definite article.

1st declension masculine nouns

All the nouns which you are about to meet end in '-ης' except for one which ends in '-ας'. Although they are all masculine in gender, note that their plural endings resemble the feminine of the definite article.

		κριτης *judge*	νεανιας *young man*
singular			
nom.	ὁ	κριτης	νεανιας
voc.	(ὦ)	κριτα	νεανια
acc.	τον	κριτην	νεανιαν
gen.	του	κριτου	νεανιου
dat.	τῳ	κριτῃ	νεανιᾳ
plural			
nom.	οἱ	κριται	νεανιαι
voc.	(ὦ)	κριται	νεανιαι
acc.	τους	κριτας	νεανιας
gen.	των	κριτων	νεανιων
dat.	τοις	κριταις	νεανιαις

Every noun with a nominative singular ending in '-ης' which you will meet in this book has endings like κριτης.

nouns like κριτης

δεσποτης	= master	πολιτης	= citizen
ναυτης	= sailor	στρατιωτης	= soldier
ποιητης	= poet		

Once you have got to know these nouns as items of vocabulary, and checked carefully the case and number of the definite article which goes before each noun, then you should not encounter much difficulty in translating sentences involving these words.

Exercise 8.1
Give the number and case of the definite article in each of these phrases. Then translate the phrase. The basic meaning of each noun is given in brackets.

1. τον δεσποτην (master)
2. οἱ ναυται (sailor)
3. τῳ πολιτῃ (citizen)
4. του κριτου (judge)
5. τους στρατιωτας (soldier)
6. των νεανιων (young man)
7. ὠ ποιητα (poet)
8. τοις δεσποταις (master)

Exercise 8.2
The nouns in this exercise have all featured in this lesson and can also be found in Vocabulary check-list 3 on the next page.

1. ὁ ποιητης γραφει.
2. οἱ νεανιαι στρατευουσιν.
3. ἀγεις τους πολιτας.
4. οὐ λυομεν τον δεσποτην.
5. ὁ κριτης παυει την μαχην.
6. ὁ δεσποτης θυει τῃ θεᾳ.
7. ὁ ποιητης γραφει ἐπιστολην.
8. οἱ στρατιωται οὐκ ἐχουσιν οἰκιας.
9. οἱ νεανιαι στρατευουσιν εἰς (into) τας ᾿Αθηνας.
10. ἀγεις τους ναυτας ἐκ (out of) της χωρας, ὠ κριτα.

Exercise 8.3
Simple word derivation questions are included on the Common Entrance paper. Translate the following Greek words into English and give an English word derived from each one.

Example: γραφω means *I write* and gives us *graphics*.

1. φωνη
2. στρατια
3. παυω
4. σοφια

Be careful to learn, from Greek to English, the words listed in Vocabulary check-list 3 on the next page before moving on further.

Revise these words carefully from Greek to English before starting the next chapter.

δεσποτης	(m.)	master
κριτης	(m.)	judge
ναυτης	(m.)	sailor
νεανιας	(m.)	young man
ποιητης	(m.)	poet
πολιτης	(m.)	citizen
στρατιωτης	(m.)	soldier
βαλλω		I throw
θεραπευω		I honour, look after, cure
λαμβανω		I take, capture
λεγω		I say, speak
μενω		I remain, wait for
παιδευω		I train, educate
σωζω		I save

The unfortunate end to Jason's quest.

CHAPTER 9

THE VERB – PRESENT TENSE OF εἰμι
USE OF THE 'GENITIVE SANDWICH'

The verb *to be* is irregular in most languages, and Greek is no exception. It is the only verb at Common Entrance Level 1 which forms its present tense in a different way from λυω.

Present tense of εἰμι

Here is the present tense of εἰμι, *I am*, in full. This verb is as common as you might expect and you need to learn it as quickly as possible. It is very easy to recite and memorise.

person	number	Greek verb	meaning
1st	singular	εἰμι	*I am*
2nd	singular	εἰ	*you are*
3rd	singular	ἐστι(ν)	*he / she / it is*
1st	plural	ἐσμεν	*we are*
2nd	plural	ἐστε	*you are*
3rd	plural	εἰσι(ν)	*they are*

The 3rd person singular and plural forms are sometimes confused. You will avoid this if you bear in mind how similar the 3rd person singular form ἐστι is to its equivalent, *est*, in Latin and French.

Exercise 9.1

Revise the present tense of εἰμι before starting this exercise.

1. εἰμι ποιητης.
2. στρατιωται ἐσμεν.
3. ἐστι δεσποτης.
4. οὐκ εἰσι κριται.
5. εἰ ἐν (in) τῃ ἀγορᾳ.
6. οὐκ ἐστε ναυται.
7. ἐσμεν ἐν (in) ταις ᾿Αθηναις.
8. ἡ θεα ἐστιν ἐν (in) τῃ χωρᾳ.
9. οὐκ εἰμι ποιητης, ὠ πολιται.
10. οὐκ εἰ κριτης ἀλλα νεανιας.

Note that when ἐστι(ν) and εἰσι(ν) come as the **first word** in a sentence, *There is . . .* and *There are . . .* are often the most suitable translations for them.

Dative of possessor

We have already learnt the verb ἐχω which means *I have*. Another common way of showing possession in Greek is by using the **3rd person** forms of εἰμι plus a noun in the dative case. Study the following example carefully:

$$\text{ἐστιν οἰκια τῳ ποιητῃ.}$$

(literally)	*There is a house to the poet.*
(good English)	*The poet has a house.*

When you come across this sort of sentence, translate it literally first and then put it into good English.

Exercise 9.2

1. ἐστιν ἀγορα τοις πολιταις.
2. τῃ θεᾳ ἐστι νικη.
3. τῳ κριτῃ ἐπιστολαι εἰσιν.
4. οὐκ ἐστι σοφια τῳ δεσποτῃ.
5. εἰσιν οἰκιαι τοις νεανιαις.

Genitive sandwich

In Greek, as in Latin, a noun in the genitive case means *of*. In the phrase *the book of the boy*, the noun *boy* would be in the genitive case. In Greek, a noun in the genitive case is usually placed **between** the noun being possessed and its article. In the above example, the Greek order of words would be *the – of the boy – book*. Study the following example carefully.

$$\text{ἡ του κριτου οἰκια.}$$

(literally)	*The – of the judge – house.*
(good English)	*The house of the judge* **or** *The judge's house.*

The genitive forms of the article του, της (singular) or των (plural), which all mean *of the*, should make your translation more easy.

Exercise 9.3

1. ἡ του πολιτου οἰκια.
2. ἡ της θεας σοφια.
3. ἡ των Ἀθηνων ἀγορα.
4. ἡ των στρατιωτων νικη.
5. οἱ της χωρας ποιηται.
6. αἱ των νεανιων φωναι.

Before you start the next chapter, read this page carefully and be sure that you know the present tense of εἰμι.

CHAPTER 10

PREPOSITIONS AND QUESTIONS

In this chapter we shall learn how to cope with longer sentences which contain prepositions, and also meet some questions for the first time.

Prepositions

The following prepositions are very common at Common Entrance and change the nouns which accompany them into one of three possible cases.

ἀπο (+ genitive)	= from
δια (+ accusative)	= because of
δια (+ genitive)	= through
εἰς (+ accusative)	= towards, into
ἐκ / ἐξ (+ genitive)	= out of (ἐξ before a vowel)
ἐν (+ dative)	= in, on
προς (+ accusative)	= towards, against

Be careful with δια which has two separate meanings depending on the case of the noun with it. If you cannot remember which case takes which meaning, learn **both** meanings as the sense of the sentence will normally tell you which one is more appropriate.

Exercise 10.1

The prepositions in this exercise are all listed above. Revise the verbs in Vocabulary check-list 3 before starting this exercise.

1. ἀπο της ἀγορας.
2. ἐν τῃ μαχῃ.
3. ἐκ της οἰκιας.
4. εἰς τας ᾿Αθηνας.
5. δια τον κριτην.
6. δια της χωρας.
7. θεραπευομεν την θεαν ἐν τῃ οἰκιᾳ.
8. βαλλει την ἐπιστολην εἰς την θαλασσαν.
9. οἱ πολιται στρατευουσιν ἐκ της γης.
10. παιδευετε τους στρατιωτας ἐν τῃ χωρᾳ.
11. ἀγω τους ναυτας προς την ἀγοραν.
12. δια την νικην ἡ στρατια σῳζει τον δεσποτην.

Questions

In English, when we want to convert a statement into a question, we usually change the verb around so that, for example, *You are going* becomes *Are you going?* In Greek, the sentence stays the same but the question word ἀρα is placed first. The Greek question mark is the same as our semi-colon (;). Study the following:

(statement)	γραφει ἐπιστολην.	= *He is writing a letter.*
(question)	ἀρα γραφει ἐπιστολην;	= *Is he writing a letter?*

Before a vowel, ἀρα frequently loses its last alpha and becomes ἀρ᾽, so that *Are the young men writing?* would become ἀρ᾽ οἱ νεανιαι γραφουσιν;

Notes on the article

Greek often includes the article with proper nouns (αἱ ᾽Αθηναι) and abstract nouns (ἡ σοφια) where we would simply say *Athens* and *wisdom*. For example, ἡ θεα ἐχει την σοφιαν would mean *The goddess has wisdom*. As always, go for the most natural English translation, but be as accurate as you can.

Exercise 10.2

1. ἀρα παυει την μαχην;
2. ἀρα σῳζεις την χωραν;
3. ἀρα λυουσι τον νεανιαν;
4. ἀρα θυετε τῃ θεᾳ;
5. ἀρ᾽ ἀγεις την στρατιαν;
6. ἀρα λαμβανει τας ᾽Αθηνας;

7. ἀρα μενεις ἐν (*in*) τῃ οἰκιᾳ, ὠ δεσποτα;
8. ἀρ᾽ οἱ ποιηται παιδευουσι τους νεανιας;
9. ἀρ᾽ οἱ πολιται εἰσιν ἐν (*in*) τῃ ἀγορᾳ;
10. ἀρα στρατευετε προς (*towards*) την θαλασσαν, ὠ στρατιωται;

Exercise 10.3

Translate the following Greek words into English and give an English word derived from each one.

1. κριτης   2. πολιτης   3. ναυτης   4. θεραπευω

Revise Vocabulary check-lists 1–3 once again, plus the present tenses of λυω and εἰμι, and the definite article ὁ / ἡ / το before moving on to Chapter 11.

CHAPTER 11

THE NOUN – 2ND DECLENSION MASCULINE AND FEMININE NOUNS

In this chapter we are going to meet some important new nouns which all end in '-oς' and belong to the Greek 2nd declension.

2nd declension masculine and feminine nouns

All the new nouns which you will meet in this chapter copy the endings of λογος, below, and are mostly masculine in gender. Note that the case endings very closely copy the masculine of the definite article.

λογος
word (m.)

singular

nom.	ὁ	λογος
voc.	(ὠ)	λογε
acc.	τον	λογον
gen.	του	λογου
dat.	τῳ	λογῳ

plural

nom.	οἱ	λογοι
voc.	(ὠ)	λογοι
acc.	τους	λογους
gen.	των	λογων
dat.	τοις	λογοις

nouns like λογος (genders are given in brackets)

Ἀθηναιος (m.)	= Athenian	ἱππος (m.)	= horse
ἀνθρωπος (m.)	= man	ὁδος (f.)	= road, way
δουλος (m.)	= slave	πολεμιοι (m. pl.)	= enemy
ἰατρος (m.)	= doctor	ποταμος (m.)	= river

You do not, at this stage, need to memorise which '-oς' nouns are masculine and which are feminine, but feminine '-oς' nouns will take the **feminine** form of the definite article: *the road* is ἡ ὁδος.

Most of these nouns appear in Vocabulary check-list 4. Once again, when you have learnt them carefully, and checked the case and number of the definite article which accompanies them, then you should find that translation work becomes quite straightforward.

Exercise 11.1

Give the gender, number and case of the definite article in each of these phrases. Then translate the phrase. The basic meaning of each noun is in brackets.

1. τον λογον   (word)
2. οἱ δουλοι   (slave)
3. τους πολεμιους   (enemy)
4. τῳ ἱππῳ   (horse)
5. των ἀνθρωπων   (man)

6. ὠ ἰατρε   (doctor)
7. της ὁδου   (road)
8. τοις ᾿Αθηναιοις (Athenian)
9. του ποταμου   (river)
10. ὠ δουλοι   (slave)

Be careful when translating the phrases for *Athens* and *the Athenians*, which are often confused. The phrase for *Athens*, αἱ ᾿Αθηναι, is **feminine**, whereas *the Athenians*, οἱ ᾿Αθηναιοι, are always **masculine**.

Exercise 11.2

New nouns in this exercise have all featured in this chapter and can also be found in Vocabulary check-list 4 on the next page.

1. λαμβανει τους ἱππους.
2. οἱ πολεμιοι στρατευουσιν.
3. λυουσι τους δουλους.
4. οἱ ᾿Αθηναιοι οὐ θυουσιν.
5. ὁ ἰατρος θεραπευει τους πολιτας.
6. οἱ στρατιωται εἰσιν ἐν (on) τῃ ὁδῳ.
7. ἐστι στρατια τοις πολεμιοις.
8. οἱ του κριτου λογοι οὐ παυουσι την μαχην.
9. ὁ δεσποτης μενει τον δουλον ἐν (in) ταις ᾿Αθηναις.
10. οἱ ᾿Αθηναιοι ἀγουσι τους ἱππους προς (towards) τον ποταμον.

Before starting the next chapter, revise and learn, from Greek to English, the words listed in Vocabulary check-list 4 on the next page.

Revise these words carefully from Greek to English before starting the next chapter.

Ἀθηναιος	(m.)	Athenian
δουλος	(m.)	slave
ἰατρος	(m.)	doctor
ἱππος	(m.)	horse
λογος	(m.)	word
ὁδος	(f.)	road, way
πολεμιοι	(m. pl.)	enemy
ποταμος	(m.)	river

ἀπο (+ gen.)	from
δια (+ acc.)	because of
δια (+ gen.)	through
εἰς (+ acc.)	towards, into
ἐκ / ἐξ (+ gen.)	out of
ἐν (+ dat.)	in, on
προς (+ acc.)	towards, against

ἀρα;	*introduces a direct question*
εἰμι	I am

The Minotaur's less fortunate half-brother, Jim.

CHAPTER 12

THE NOUN – 2ND DECLENSION NEUTER NOUNS

In this chapter you will come across a small, but important, group of 2nd declension nouns which are all neuter in gender.

2nd declension neuter nouns

All the neuter nouns which you will meet in this book end in '–ον' and change their endings like δωρον, below. Note that the case endings are the same as the neuter form of the definite article, except for the nominative, vocative and accusative singular.

$$\delta\omega\rho\text{ον}$$
gift

singular

nom.	το	δωρον
voc.	(ὠ)	δωρον
acc.	το	δωρον
gen.	του	δωρου
dat.	τῳ	δωρῳ

plural

nom.	τα	δωρα
voc.	(ὠ)	δωρα
acc.	τα	δωρα
gen.	των	δωρων
dat.	τοις	δωροις

nouns like δωρον

δενδρον	= tree	ὁπλα (pl.)	= weapons
ἐργον	= work, action	πλοιον	= boat
ζῳον	= animal	τεκνον	= child

Neuter plural takes a singular verb

One odd feature of Greek which you will come across is that subjects which are neuter plural take 3rd person **singular** verbs with them. For *The boats are in the sea*, Greek says *The boats is in the sea*, or τα πλοια ἐστιν ἐν τῃ θαλασσῃ. However, the article will tell you whether a neuter subject is singular (το) or plural (τα).

Exercise 12.1

Give the number and case of the definite article in each of these phrases. Then translate the phrase. Give more than one case if appropriate. The basic meaning of each noun is given in brackets.

1. τοῦ δωρου *(gift)*
2. τα πλοια *(boat)*
3. τῳ δενδρῳ *(tree)*
4. τοις ὁπλοις *(weapons)*

5. τῳ ἐργῳ *(work)*
6. ὠ τεκνον *(child)*
7. τοῦ ζῳου *(animal)*
8. το πλοιον *(boat)*

Dative of instrument

It is worth remembering at this point that the dative case, in Greek, as well as meaning *to* and *for* can also mean *by* or *with* (non-living things). This **instrumental** use of the dative is less common, but can sometimes be the only correct translation, as in παιδευομεν τα τεκνα τῃ σοφιᾳ, *We train the children with wisdom.* In translation work, write whatever makes the best sense to you.

Exercise 12.2

New nouns in this exercise have all featured in this chapter and can also be found in Vocabulary check-list 5 on the next page.

1. λυετε τα ζῳα.
2. το τεκνον γραφει.
3. ἐχομεν το δωρον.
4. οὐκ ἐστι δενδρα ἐν τῃ ἀγορᾳ.
5. τα τεκνα λαμβανει τον ἱππον.
6. οὐκ ἐστιν ὁπλα τῃ στρατιᾳ.
7. ἀρ᾽ οἱ ἰατροι θεραπευουσι τα τεκνα;
8. τα των στρατιωτων ἐργα σῳζει τας Ἀθηνας.
9. οἱ ναυται βαλλουσι τα ὁπλα εἰς το πλοιον.
10. οἱ δουλοι θεραπευουσι την θεαν τοις δωροις.

Exercise 12.3

Translate the following Greek words into English and give an English word derived from each one.

1. ἱππος
2. λογος
3. ἰατρος
4. βαλλω

Do revise Vocabulary check-list 5 carefully before starting Chapter 13, as it contains some nouns which will be new to you.

Revise these words carefully from Greek to English before starting the next chapter.

ἀνθρωπος	(m.)	man
βαρβαροι	(m. pl.)	barbarians
βιβλος	(f.)	book
βιος	(m.)	life
δημος	(m.)	people
θεος	(m.)	god
δενδρον	(n.)	tree
δωρον	(n.)	gift
ἐργον	(n.)	work, action
ζῳον	(n.)	animal
ὁπλα	(n. pl.)	weapons
πλοιον	(n.)	boat
τεκνον	(n.)	child

'To Cyclops, Happy Birthday from Poseidon'

CHAPTER 13

THE VERB – IMPERFECT TENSE OF λυω

The imperfect tense is the only past tense which you need to know for Level 1 of Common Entrance, and it is only found on question 2 of the paper, which is the short passage of unseen translation.

How to identify the imperfect tense

The imperfect tense is usually translated as *was* or *were* doing something. As well as employing separate imperfect tense endings, Greek also adds an epsilon to the **front** of the verb to indicate that a past tense is being used. This is called an **augment.** Study the imperfect tense of λυω, below, and bear in mind that all the verbs which you will be required to translate in this book, form their imperfect tenses in the same way. Hyphens have been put in to indicate the additions before and after the verb stem.

person	number	Greek verb	meaning
1st	singular	ἐ-λυ-ον	*I was setting free*
2nd	singular	ἐ-λυ-ες	*you were setting free*
3rd	singular	ἐ-λυ-ε(ν)	*he / she / it was setting free*
1st	plural	ἐ-λυ-ομεν	*we were setting free*
2nd	plural	ἐ-λυ-ετε	*you were setting free*
3rd	plural	ἐ-λυ-ον	*they were setting free*

Try to memorise the imperfect tense of λυω as quickly as you can. Note that the 1st person singular and 3rd person plural forms are identical; the sense of the sentence will make it clear which of the two meanings is more appropriate.

Exercise 13.1

Practise saying the imperfect tenses of the following new verbs in full. They all copy the pattern of λυω. Hyphens have been included to show you where the endings should be added.

1. διωκ-ω   (*I pursue*)
2. κωλυ-ω   (*I obstruct*)
3. πειθ-ω   (*I persuade*)
4. πεμπ-ω   (*I send*)
5. φευγ-ω   (*I run away*)
6. φυλασσ-ω   (*I guard*)

Exercise 13.2

A mixture of verbs in the present and imperfect tenses. Translate each verb and indicate whether it is present or imperfect tense. For some verbs there may be more than one correct translation.

1. βαλλει.
2. ἐβαλλεν.
3. ἐγραφες.
4. γραφεις.
5. ἐλεγετε.

6. λεγετε.
7. ἐπαιδευον.
8. ἐθυομεν.
9. ἐστιν.
10. ἐχουσιν.

Exercise 13.3

1. ἐπαυομεν την μαχην.
2. οἱ νεανιαι ἐστρατευον.
3. ἐπαιδευε τα τεκνα.
4. οὐκ ἐμενετε ἐν τῃ οἰκιᾳ.
5. ὁ δημος ἐθυε τοις θεοις.
6. ἐγραφες λογους ἐν τῃ βιβλῳ.
7. οἱ του κριτου λογοι ἐσῳζον το τεκνον.
8. οἱ δουλοι ἐλυον τα ζῳα ἀπο της οἰκιας.
9. ἡ στρατια ἐστρατευεν ἐκ της των βαρβαρων χωρας.
10. οἱ Ἀθηναιοι ἐθεραπευον τον ποιητην δια την σοφιαν.

Exercise 13.4

Translate the following Greek words into English and give an English word derived from each one.

1. βιβλος   2. βιος   3. δημος   4. ζῳον

Before you go any further, make sure that you can recite the imperfect tense of λυω without looking up any of its parts. Please also ensure that you have learnt the contents of Vocabulary check-list 6, which contains the remainder of the nouns on the Common Entrance list.

Vocabulary check-list 6

Revise these words carefully from Greek to English before starting the next chapter.

ἀδελφος	(m.)	brother
ἡλιος	(m.)	sun
θανατος	(m.)	death
κινδυνος	(m.)	danger
νησος	(f.)	island
νοσος	(f.)	disease
ξενος	(m.)	friend, stranger
στρατηγος	(m.)	general
ὑπνος	(m.)	sleep

διωκω	I pursue
κωλυω	I obstruct, prevent
πειθω	I persuade
πεμπω	I send
φευγω	I run away
φυλασσω	I guard

The somewhat less famous story of the Trojan Rabbit.

CHAPTER 14

ADJECTIVES

Adjectives in English do not usually change their appearance in any way to match the word which they describe. The word *good*, for example, can be used to describe any number of people, be they masculine or feminine, without any alteration to its spelling. However, in Greek, as in Latin, adjectives change their ending to match the **gender**, **number** and **case** of the person or thing they describe.

The adjective σοφος

Study the various forms of σοφος, below. Although there appears to be a lot to take in all at once, notice that most of the endings copy the equivalent forms of the definite article.

σοφος, *wise*

	masculine	feminine	neuter
singular			
nom.	σοφος	σοφη	σοφον
voc.	σοφε	σοφη	σοφον
acc.	σοφον	σοφην	σοφον
gen.	σοφου	σοφης	σοφου
dat.	σοφῳ	σοφῃ	σοφῳ
plural			
nom.	σοφοι	σοφαι	σοφα
voc.	σοφοι	σοφαι	σοφα
acc.	σοφους	σοφας	σοφα
gen.	σοφων	σοφων	σοφων
dat.	σοφοις	σοφαις	σοφοις

At the moment it is far more important that you learn each adjective as a piece of vocabulary rather than try to recite all its endings automatically.

adjectives like σοφος

ἀγαθος = good   καλος   = beautiful, fine
δεινος = strange, terrible   χαλεπος = difficult, dangerous
κακος = bad

Use and position of adjectives

The adjective is usually found between the article and its noun, as in English. For example, *the good slave* would be ὁ ἀγαθος δουλος. Without the article, ἀγαθος δουλος would mean *a good slave*.

The article is often used with adjectives to show a class of people, for example οἱ ἀγαθοι, *the good* **or** *good men* and οἱ κακοι, *the bad* **or** *bad men*.

Exercise 14.1

Translate the phrases and give the gender, number and case of the adjective in each one. The basic meaning of each adjective is in brackets. Give more than one case if appropriate.

1. ὁ σοφος (*wise*) κριτης.
2. τον ἀγαθον (*good*) ναυτην.
3. αἱ δειναι (*strange, terrible*) φωναι.
4. της χαλεπης (*difficult, dangerous*) ὁδου.
5. τα κακα (*bad*) τεκνα.
6. ταις καλαις (*beautiful, fine*) νησοις.

Exercise 14.2

The adjectives used are all taken from **Exercise 14.1**

1. ὁ νεανιας ἐστι σοφος.
2. ἐστε ἀγαθοι πολιται.
3. αἱ Ἀθηναι εἰσι καλαι.
4. ἐθυες τῳ δεινῳ θεῳ.
5. ἐστι καλη νικη τοις Ἀθηναιοις.
6. τα ὁπλα ἐστι χαλεπα και δεινα.
7. τα του στρατηγου ἐργα ἐστιν ἀγαθα.
8. οἱ κακοι οὐ κωλυουσι τους πολεμιους.
9. εἰσι δεινοι κινδυνοι ἐν τῳ ποταμῳ.
10. ὁ δεσποτης ἐπειθε τους δουλους σοφοις λογοις.

Exercise 14.3

Translate the following Greek words into English and give an English word derived from each one.

1. ὑπνος   2. ἡλιος   3. στρατηγος   4. φευγω

The adjective φιλιος

Adjectives which end in '-ιος' or '-ρος', like φιλιος, below, replace the eta (η) with an alpha (α) in their feminine singular forms, but are otherwise similar to σοφος.

φιλιος, friendly

	masculine	feminine	neuter
singular			
nom.	φιλιος	φιλια	φιλιον
voc.	φιλιε	φιλια	φιλιον
acc.	φιλιον	φιλιαν	φιλιον
gen.	φιλιου	φιλιας	φιλιου
dat.	φιλιω	φιλια	φιλιω

The plural forms, φιλιοι, φιλιαι, φιλια etc. change their endings precisely like σοφοι, σοφαι, σοφα, the plural of σοφος.

adjectives like φιλιος

ἀνδρειος   = brave   μακρος = long
δικαιος   = just, right   μικρος = small

Exercise 14.4

The adjectives used are all listed above.

1. οὐκ ἐστε φιλιοι.
2. ἡ ἡμερα ἐστι μακρα.
3. οἱ ἀδελφοι εἰσιν ἀνδρειοι.
4. σῳζομεν τα μικρα ζῳα.
5. ὁ ξενος λεγει φιλιᾳ φωνῃ.
6. οἱ του κριτου λογοι εἰσι δικαιοι.
7. ἐστι τῳ ναυτῃ μικρον πλοιον.
8. οἱ πολιται ἐφυλασσον την μικραν νησον.
9. οἱ βαρβαροι οὐκ εἰσι φιλιοι τοις Ἀθηναιοις.
10. ἀρα διωκεις τους πολεμιους προς την μακραν ὁδον;

All the adjectives in this chapter are listed in Vocabulary check-list 7, which contains the last of the words which you need to know for Common Entrance Level 1. Please learn them carefully before moving on to Chapter 15.

Revise these words carefully from Greek to English before starting the next chapter.

ἀγγελλω	I announce
βλαπτω	I harm, damage
ἀγαθος	good
ἀνδρειος	brave
δεινος	strange, terrible, clever
δικαιος	just, right
κακος	bad
καλος	beautiful, fine
μακρος	long
μικρος	small
σοφος	wise
φιλιος	friendly
χαλεπος	difficult, dangerous
νυν	now

CHAPTER 15

THE VERB – FUTURE TENSE OF $\lambda\upsilon\omega$

The future tense is, like the imperfect tense, only found on the second, and final, question of Common Entrance Level 1, which is the short passage of unseen translation. Fortunately for us, it is an easy tense to identify and remember.

How to identify the future tense

The future tense is usually translated as *shall* or *will* do something. Greek forms the future tense simply by adding a sigma (σ) between the verb stem and its present tense endings. Study the future tense of $\lambda\upsilon\omega$, which is set out below. All the verbs which you will be required to translate in this book form their future tenses in the same way, apart from a few exceptions which we shall meet later. Hyphens have been put in to show the future tense endings on the verb stem '$\lambda\upsilon$-'.

person	number	Greek verb	meaning
1st	singular	$\lambda\upsilon$-$\sigma\omega$	*I shall set free*
2nd	singular	$\lambda\upsilon$-$\sigma\epsilon\iota\varsigma$	*you will set free*
3rd	singular	$\lambda\upsilon$-$\sigma\epsilon\iota$	*he / she / it will set free*
1st	plural	$\lambda\upsilon$-$\sigma o\mu\epsilon\nu$	*we shall set free*
2nd	plural	$\lambda\upsilon$-$\sigma\epsilon\tau\epsilon$	*you will set free*
3rd	plural	$\lambda\upsilon$-$\sigma o\upsilon\sigma\iota(\nu)$	*they will set free*

You will obviously not find this a difficult tense to memorise if you can remember the present tense of $\lambda\upsilon\omega$, but be careful not to confuse the present and future tenses, which look very similar. Remember that future tenses are **only** found on **question 2** of the paper, and usually inside direct speech or speech marks.

Exercise 15.1

Practise saying the future tenses of the following verbs in full, and also give their basic meanings in English. Hyphens have been included to show where the endings should be added.

1. $\theta\upsilon$-ω.   3. $\kappa\omega\lambda\upsilon$-$\omega$.   5. $\theta\epsilon\rho\alpha\pi\epsilon\upsilon$-$\omega$.
2. $\pi\alpha\upsilon$-ω.   4. $\pi\alpha\iota\delta\epsilon\upsilon$-$\omega$.   6. $\sigma\tau\rho\alpha\tau\epsilon\upsilon$-$\omega$.

Irregular future tense forms

Verbs which end in -$\gamma\omega$, -$\kappa\omega$, -$\sigma\omega$ and -$\chi\omega$ change to -$\xi\omega$ in their future tense forms, which otherwise copy the endings of $\lambda\upsilon\sigma\omega$.

ἀγω *(I lead)* ► ἀξω *(I shall lead)*
διωκω *(I pursue)* ► διωξω *(I shall pursue)*
ἐχω *(I have)* ► ἑξω *(I shall have)*
λεγω *(I say)* ► λεξω *(I shall say)*
φυλασσω *(I guard)* ► φυλαξω *(I shall guard)*

Verbs which end in -πω, -πτω and -φω change to -ψω in their future tense forms. σῳζω converts the -ζω to -σω.

βλαπτω *(I harm)* ► βλαψω *(I shall harm)*
γραφω *(I write)* ► γραψω *(I shall write)*
πεμπω *(I send)* ► πεμψω *(I shall send)*
σῳζω *(I save)* ► σωσω *(I shall save)*

Note how the '-so' sound in the future tense is preserved by the consonants ξ (= ks) and ψ (= ps).

Exercise 15.2

1. ὁ δουλος γραψει.
2. θυσομεν τα ζῳα.
3. ἀξεις τους νεανιας.
4. ἡ θεα φυλαξει τας Ἀθηνας.
5. σωσετε τα των πολιτων τεκνα.
6. βλαψει την στρατιαν δεινοις ὁπλοις.
7. ὁ ἀδελφος πεμψει μικραν ἐπιστολην.
8. ἡ θαλασσα οὐ κωλυσει τους πολεμιους.
9. νυν στρατευσουσιν εἰς τον χαλεπον ποταμον.
10. ἀρ' ὁ ἀγαθος ἰατρος θεραπευσει την δεινην νοσον;

Exercise 15.3

Translate the following Greek words into English and give an English word derived from each one.

1. ἀγγελλω   2. δεινος   3. μικρος   4. φιλιος

Well done for reaching the end of the final chapter. Revise Vocabulary check-lists 4–7 once again, plus the imperfect and future tenses of λυω, before trying the practice Common Entrance questions.

PRACTICE UNSEEN PASSAGES

On question two of the Common Entrance Level 1 paper you will have to translate a small passage of Greek. You can expect to find imperfect tenses used regularly here, as well as future tenses if direct speech is involved. Verbs which introduce direct speech are generally followed by a colon, marked · in Greek. In the interests of good translation, don't be afraid to translate the article as *his*, *her*, *its* or *their* rather than *the* if the sense demands it – this possessive usage is quite common in Greek.

Make sure you revise the grammar and vocabulary contained in Chapters 1–15 carefully before attempting these passages, which are worth 25 marks each. Read the title and passage carefully before attempting a translation; names mentioned in the title are generally not given again on the right as separate items of vocabulary. When translating, you should put the glossed words *and*, *however*, *for* and *therefore* as the **first word** in any sentence where they occur.

Exercise 16.1

The musician Arion is saved from death by a dolphin.

ὁ Ἀριων ἦν ἀγαθος κιθαρῳδος και
ἐπαιδευε τους νεανιας. ἀλλα κακοι ναυται
ἐβαλλον τον Ἀριονα ἐκ πλοιου εἰς την
θαλασσαν. φιλιος μεντοι δελφις ἐσῳζε τον
ἀνθρωπον.

ἦν = was
κιθαρῳδος = musician

Ἀριονα = acc. of Ἀριων

μεντοι = however
δελφις = dolphin

Exercise 16.2

The Athenians escape from the invading Persians.

οἱ Περσαι ἐστρατευον προς τας Ἀθηνας. οἱ
δε Ἀθηναιοι οὐκ ἐσῳζον τας οἰκιας ἀλλ᾽
ἐφευγον εἰς μικραν νησον. και ἐλεγον·
"ἀρα παυσομεν τα των πολεμιων πλοια;"

Περσαι = Persians

δε = and

Exercise 16.3

Jason gathers a crew to search for the golden fleece.

ὁ Ἰασων <u>ἠν</u> ἀνδρειος νεανιας. ἐλεγε <u>δε</u>   ἠν = was
δε = and

τοις πολιταις· "ἀξω ἀγαθους ναυτας δια

χαλεπων θαλασσων και ἑξω την νικην."

<u>οὑτως</u> ἐπειθε τους πολιτας φιλιοις λογοις.   οὑτως = in this way

Exercise 16.4

The Athenians decide to attack the island of Sicily.

οἱ Ἀθηναιοι ἐστρατευον προς τους

πολεμιους. οἱ <u>δε</u> στρατηγοι ἐλεγον·   δε = and

"δικαιον ἐστι <u>λαμβανειν</u> την <u>Σικελιαν</u>.   λαμβανειν = to capture
Σικελιαν = Sicily

οἱ <u>γαρ</u> πολεμιοι πεμπουσι πλοια εἰς την   γαρ = for

νησον."

ἐπειθον <u>οὐν</u> τους πολιτας.   οὐν = therefore

Exercise 16.5

Heracles with difficulty defeats the Nemean lion.

ὁ Ἡρακλης ἐδιωκε τον <u>λεοντα</u> δια χαλεπης   λεοντα = lion

χωρας. ἐβλαπτεν <u>αὐτον</u> δεινοις ὁπλοις ἀλλ'   αὐτον = it

ὁ <u>λεων</u> οὐκ ἐφευγεν.   λεων = lion

<u>τελος</u> δε ὁ Ἡρακλης ἐθυε το ζῳον τῃ των   τελος = at last
δε = and

Ἀθηνων θεᾳ.

PRACTICE COMMON ENTRANCE LEVEL 1 PAPER

This practice paper will give you an idea of what to expect at Common Entrance Level 1. Only try it when you have revised Chapters 1–15 thoroughly. You should spend no longer than 60 minutes on this paper, and, if you are treating it as serious examination practice, you should not look up any words. Good luck.

1. (a) Write the following Greek words in English letters.
   (i) Περσευς
   (ii) τραυμα
   (iii) Ὀλυμπος
   (iv) Γεωργος
   (v) Βρεταννια (10)

   (b) Write the following English words in Greek letters.
   (i) Troia
   (ii) exodos
   (iii) Syria
   (iv) arōma
   (v) Aphroditē (10)

   (c) Translate the following Greek words into English and give an English word derived from each one.
   (i) γραφω
   (ii) βιος
   (iii) δημος
   (iv) μικρος
   (v) παυω (10)

   (d) Translate the following Greek verbs.
   (i) λυεις
   (ii) μενουσι
   (iii) λεγομεν
   (iv) ἀγετε
   (v) εἰμι (10)

(e) Translate the following sentences.

(i) ἀγομεν την στρατιαν.

(ii) λυει τον ἱππον.

(iii) οἱ δουλοι γραφουσιν.

(iv) οὐκ ἐχω οἰκιαν.

(v) τα τεκνα ἐστι φιλια.   (15)

(f) Translate the following sentences.

(i) στρατευεις ἐκ της δεινης χωρας.

(ii) ἀρ' ἐχεις την ἐπιστολην ἐν τῃ οἰκιᾳ;

(iii) ὁ των πολιτων βιος ἐστιν ἀγαθος.

(iv) ὁ κριτης λεγει σοφους λογους.

(v) τοις πολεμιοις ἐστι μικρα πλοια.   (20)

2. Translate the following passage.

The Athenians adopt Athena as the goddess of their city.

ἡ 'Αθηνα ἦν θεα της σοφιας. οἱ οὖν   ἦν = was
                                           οὖν = therefore
'Αθηναιοι ἐθεραπευον την 'Αθηναν και

ἐλεγον· "ἡ θεα οὐκ ἐστι δεινη ἀλλ' ἀγαθη.

φυλαξει γαρ τους πολιτας."   γαρ = for

                                                     (25)

Now check your work carefully.

(Total marks: 100)

GRAMMAR SUMMARY

The definite article (*the*)

sing.	masc.	fem.	neut.	plur.	masc.	fem.	neut.
nom.	ὁ	ἡ	το		οἱ	αἱ	τα
acc.	τον	την	το		τους	τας	τα
gen.	του	της	του		των	των	των
dat.	τῳ	τῃ	τῳ		τοις	ταις	τοις

Nouns in the vocative case are usually introduced by ὦ (*O*).

Nouns – 1st declension

	victory (f.)	country (f.)	sea (f.)	judge (m.)	young man (m.)
sing.					
nom.	νικη	χωρα	θαλασσα	κριτης	νεανιας
voc.	νικη	χωρα	θαλασσα	κριτα	νεανια
acc.	νικην	χωραν	θαλασσαν	κριτην	νεανιαν
gen.	νικης	χωρας	θαλασσης	κριτου	νεανιου
dat.	νικῃ	χωρᾳ	θαλασσῃ	κριτῃ	νεανιᾳ
plur.					
nom.	νικαι	χωραι	θαλασσαι	κριται	νεανιαι
voc.	νικαι	χωραι	θαλασσαι	κριται	νεανιαι
acc.	νικας	χωρας	θαλασσας	κριτας	νεανιας
gen.	νικων	χωρων	θαλασσων	κριτων	νεανιων
dat.	νικαις	χωραις	θαλασσαις	κριταις	νεανιαις

In this book, **all** nouns in '-α' change endings like χωρα except for θαλασσα whose genitive and dative singular forms are slightly different.

48

Nouns – 2nd declension

	word (m.)	gift (n.)
sing.		
nom.	λογος	δωρον
voc.	λογε	δωρον
acc.	λογον	δωρον
gen.	λογου	δωρου
dat.	λογῳ	δωρῳ
plur.		
nom.	λογοι	δωρα
voc.	λογοι	δωρα
acc.	λογους	δωρα
gen.	λογων	δωρων
dat.	λογοις	δωροις

The following nouns end in '-ος' and are feminine in gender: βιβλος *book*, ὁδος *road, way*, νησος *island* and νοσος *disease*.

Adjectives

Refer to Chapter 14 for full information on adjectives.

Verb tenses of λυω (*I set free*) and εἰμι (*I am*)

		λυω present	λυω future	λυω imperfect	εἰμι present
sing.	1st	λυω	λυσω	ἐλυον	εἰμι
	2nd	λυεις	λυσεις	ἐλυες	εἰ
	3rd	λυει	λυσει	ἐλυε(ν)	ἐστι(ν)
plur.	1st	λυομεν	λυσομεν	ἐλυομεν	ἐσμεν
	2nd	λυετε	λυσετε	ἐλυετε	ἐστε
	3rd	λυουσι(ν)	λυσουσι(ν)	ἐλυον	εἰσι(ν)

The future and imperfect tenses are required **only** for question 2 of the Common Entrance Level 1 paper.

VOCABULARY

ἀγαθος	good	εἰμι	I am
ἀγγελλω	I announce	εἰς (+ acc.)	towards, into
ἀγορα (f.)	market-place	εἰσι / εἰσιν	(they) are
ἀγω	I lead	ἐκ (+ gen.)	out of
ἀδελφος (m.)	brother	ἐν (+ dat.)	in, on
Ἀθηναι (f. pl.)	Athens	ἐξ (+ gen.)	out of
Ἀθηναιος (m.)	Athenian	ἐξω (fut.)	I shall have, hold
ἀλλα / ἀλλ'	but	ἐπιστολη (f.)	letter
ἀνδρειος	brave	ἐργον (n.)	work, action
ἀνθρωπος (m.)	man	ἐστι / ἐστιν	(he/she/it) is
ἀξω (fut.)	I shall lead	ἐχω	I have, hold
ἀπο (+ gen.)	from		
ἀρα / ἀρ'	*introduces a direct question*	ζῳον (n.)	animal
βαλλω	I throw	ἡ	the (*fem.*)
βαρβαροι (m. pl.)	barbarians	ἡλιος (m.)	sun
βιβλος (f.)	book	ἡμερα (f.)	day
βιος (m.)	life		
βλαπτω	I harm, damage	θαλασσα (f.)	sea
βλαψω (fut.)	I shall harm, damage	θανατος (m.)	death
		θεα (f.)	goddess
γη (f.)	land	θεος (m.)	god
γραφω	I write	θεραπευω	I honour, look after, cure
γραψω (fut.)	I shall write	θυω	I sacrifice
δεινος	strange, terrible, clever	ἰατρος (m.)	doctor
δενδρον (n.)	tree	ἱππος (m.)	horse
δεσποτης (m.)	master		
δημος (m.)	people	και	and
δια (+ acc.)	because of	κακος	bad
δια (+ gen.)	through	καλος	beautiful, fine
δικαιος	just, right	κινδυνος (m.)	danger
διωκω	I pursue	κριτης (m.)	judge
διωξω (fut.)	I shall pursue	κωλυω	I obstruct, prevent
δουλος (m.)	slave		
δωρον (n.)	gift		

λαμβανω	I take, capture	πεμπω	I send
λεγω	I say, speak	πεμψω (fut.)	I shall send
λεξω (fut.)	I shall say, speak	πλοιον (n.)	boat
λογος (m.)	word	ποιητης (m.)	poet
λυω	I set free	πολεμιοι (m. pl.)	enemy
		πολιτης (m.)	citizen
μακρος	long	ποταμος (m.)	river
μαχη (f.)	battle	προς (+ acc.)	towards, against
μενω	I remain, wait for		
μικρος	small	σοφια (f.)	wisdom
		σοφος	wise
ναυτης (m.)	sailor	στρατευω	I march
νεανιας (m.)	young man	στρατηγος (m.)	general
νησος (f.)	island	στρατια (f.)	army
νικη (f.)	victory	στρατιωτης (m.)	soldier
νοσος (f.)	disease	σωζω	I save
νυν	now	σωσω (fut.)	I shall save
ξενος (m.)	friend, stranger	τεκνον (n.)	child
		το	the (neut.)
ὁ	the (masc.)		
ὁδος (f.)	road, way	ὑπνος (m.)	sleep
οἰκια (f.)	house		
ὁπλα (n. pl.)	weapons	φευγω	I run away
οὐ	not	φιλιος	friendly
οὐκ (+ smooth breathing)	not	φυλασσω	I guard
		φυλαξω (fut.)	I shall guard
οὐχ (+ rough breathing)	not	φωνη (f.)	voice
		χαλεπος	difficult, dangerous
παιδευω	I train, educate	χωρα (f.)	country
παυω	I stop		
πειθω	I persuade	ὠ (+ voc.)	O